Early Advanced Piano

T0016962

Christmas Carols

Arranged by DAVID GLEN HATCH

10 Solo Piano Arrangements of Traditional Carols

Music of Christmas is magic to the ears, providing joyful memories for many years. This volume celebrates a variety of beloved Christmas carols with advanced arrangements that capture a range of styles, textures, colors, and harmonies—from a "Deck the Halls" hoedown to a jazz rendition of "Fum, Fum, Fum." The exotic sounds of "We Three Kings of Orient Are," the ringing church chimes of "Silent Night," the somber elegance of "O Come, O Come Emmanuel," and all the other wonderful musical moments are certain to provide hours of enjoyment for the pianist who wishes to be a *Popular Performer*.

CONTENTS

Alfred Music
P.O. Box 10003
Van Nuys, CA 91410-0003
alfred.com

ISBN-10: 1-4706-4263-8
ISBN-13: 978-1-4706-4263-1

Cover Photo: Ornament © Getty Images

A Christmas of Joy
(The First Noel / Angels We Have Heard On High / Joy to the World / O Come, All Ye Faithful)

Arr. David Glen Hatch

"Angels We Have Heard On High"
Traditional French Melody
Joyfully (♩ = 112)

Più mosso (♩ = 120)

chime-like

cresc. e rit.

"Joy to the World"
Lowell Mason

Meno mosso (♩ = 112)
"O Come, All Ye Faithful"
John Francis Wade

COVENTRY CAROL

Traditional English Carol
Arr. David Glen Hatch

Deck the Halls

Traditional Welsh Carol
Arr. David Glen Hatch

Gaily, with a bounce (♩ = 84)

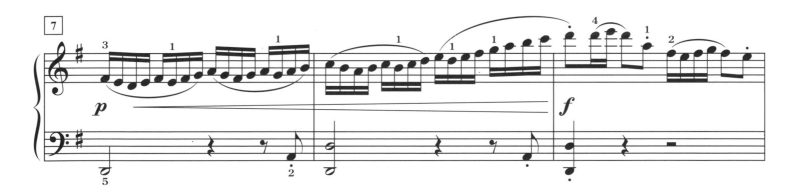

Fum, Fum, Fum

Traditional
Arr. David Glen Hatch

Brightly, like a sizzling jazz improvization ($\quad$ = 120)

God Rest Ye Merry, Gentlemen

Traditional English Carol
Arr. David Glen Hatch

I Saw Three Ships

Traditional English Carol
Arr. David Glen Hatch

O Come, O Come Emmanuel

Plainsong
Arr. David Glen Hatch

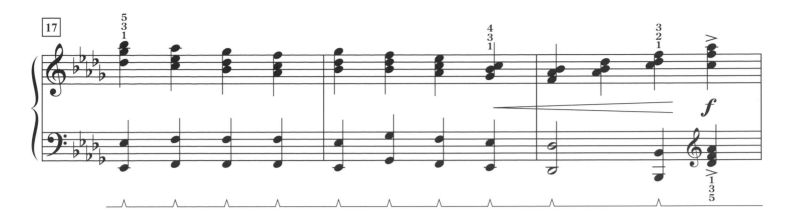

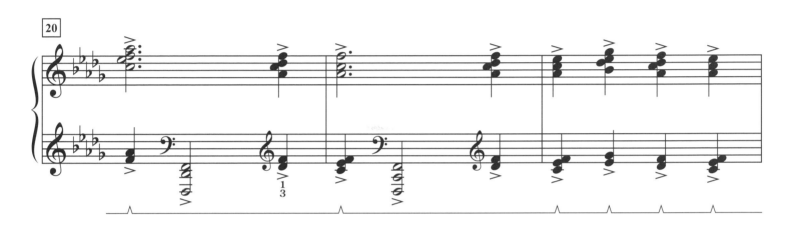

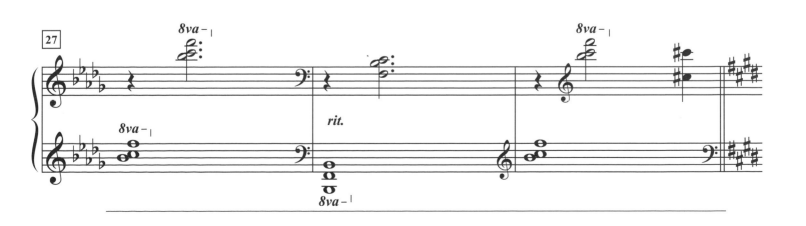

Silent Night

Franz Grüber
Arr. David Glen Hatch

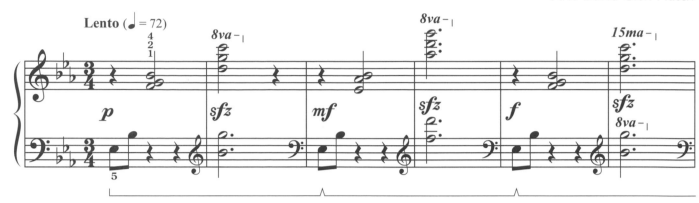

WE THREE KINGS OF ORIENT ARE

John Henry Hopkins, Jr.
Arr. David Glen Hatch

Still, Still, Still

Traditional Austrian Carol
Arr. David Glen Hatch